AF326609

A RETURN ON WELLNESS

ROW

YOUR BUSINESS TO HEALTH

ELIZABETH BLACKLEY

Copyright © Elizabeth Blackley 2026

First published by Hembury Books in 2026

hemburybooks.com.au

info@hemburybooks.com

ISBN 9781923765016 (hardback)

ISBN 9781923765023 (ebook)

A catalogue record for this book is available from the National Library of Australia

This publication is intended for informational purposes only. The author and publisher disclaim any liability arising from the use or misuse of the content.

Ethical use technology

Technology tools were leveraged to support research in alignment with corporate standards for responsible and ethical technology use. The author wrote this book.

For permissions or inquiries, contact: tellmemore@neoconnections.com.au.

For those who wish to design work that sustains people.

'To live is the rarest thing in the world.
Most people exist, that is all.'

— Oscar Wilde —

CONTENTS

Foreword

Films are like start-ups: high-stakes gambles to make widely adopted, often expensive-to-create consumer products in a very compressed amount of time. I have experience in each of these. Both work environments are intriguing Petri dishes for observing teams in extreme conditions to see how they – and their leaders – rise to the occasion or fracture.

Elizabeth digs into many of the phenomena we've all witnessed at work: healthy versus toxic stress, burnout, fatigue, distributed (often asynchronous) teamwork and return-to-office mandates. The book you are about to read is nothing if not topical.

From working at three motion-picture studios on titles as varied as *Die Hard 5* and *The Wolverine to Independence Day and Braveheart*, and founding three start-ups, including both successful exits and failures, I've worked side by side with high performers who've found sustainable ways to serve as both contributors and as leaders – and also with those who burned out and left for a stress-free life.

What fascinated me, even early on, was not that these environments in which we worked were stressful. That was obvious.

What fascinated me was how differently people responded to that stress over time, and what the early predictors of individual and team success were.

In retrospect, some of the most talented people with whom I worked in my 20s – directors, producers, founders, engineers, creators – had left for other industries by my 30s. The ones who stayed and thrived usually had a role model, either a leader or a mentor, who taught them how to be fully present under pressure without being consumed by it, how to create sustainable work practices and how to recover from setbacks.

Learning early that knowing how to navigate the volatile and stressful modern workplace was the key to surviving – and winning.

Elizabeth's book sits squarely in that tension. I love how she traces how our modern understanding of work – shaped by industrial efficiency, corporate competition and now digital acceleration – has normalised chronic stress while treating burnout as an individual failure rather than a systemic signal.

Historically, we have celebrated endurance and sacrifice, often mistaking depletion for dedication. We are now acknowledging the crisis of a culture that extracts *and values* short-term performance at the expense of long-term human capacity.

I warn you now: this is not your typical business book in the point-of-sale rack of some duty-free bookstore for passing travellers. Elizabeth's editors did not force her to pad this out to hundreds of pages of colourful anecdotes just to justify a price point. This is a dense read where each sentence carries its weight, and citations and footnotes offer opportunities to go even deeper across neuroscience, psychology, contemplative traditions and practical workplace experimentation.

When you finish, one thing will be clear: Elizabeth is passionate about giving us more than just a roadmap to the history of work or a screed on modern stress. Rather, she offers us a vision of a workplace that recognises focus as a finite resource and treats rest, recovery and emotional regulation as performance enablers rather than as indulgences.

In both film and technology, I eventually learned that the best outcomes rarely came from maximal force. They came from creating conditions where deep focus – what many call flow – could reliably occur.

Flow is not mystical. It is a neurobiological state in which challenge and skill are balanced, distractions are minimised, and the mind is fully engaged in the task at hand. It is also, not coincidentally, the state in which people report the highest levels of satisfaction with their work. I am so passionate about making flow states accessible to modern knowledge workers that I run a company with just this goal.

The teams whose leaders create conditions for this state through clear goals, protected attention, psychological safety and humane pacing consistently outperform those who rely on adrenaline and willpower alone. They ship better products, make fewer catastrophic errors and, perhaps most importantly, they are still curious, healthy and motivated years later.

What makes this book valuable is that it situates modern workplace practices within a longer human context. It does not offer one single prescription. Stress, effort and meaning have always been intertwined. What has changed is scale, speed and the degree to which work now follows us everywhere.

By examining both the history and the lived consequences of these shifts, Elizabeth invites us to be more intentional about how we work and how we create workplace culture, to consider that we not merely grind harder mindlessly.

This said, with a book this concise, it would be disrespectful to write too long a foreword, and, unlike Pascal, I did have a moment to make it shorter. So, let's get to the good stuff, shall we? Wellbeing that works ... awaits.

Steven Puri
Founder, The Sukha Company
Austin, Texas
February 2026

Many truths, one direction

The following fable invites reflection on what unfolds when different perspectives meet. It illustrates the complexity that arises when varied beliefs and ways of working converge, and the patience required to navigate those differences. It also reminds us that every voice carries something of value.

In workplaces, this truth matters: progress depends on recognising diversity of thought and experience, then finding ways to align those differences towards shared goals. As you read, you are invited to consider how the story mirrors the challenge and opportunity of creating environments where many truths can move in one direction. The ability to pause – to step back, listen and create space for understanding – is often what makes that alignment possible.

* * *

In the quiet grove of Whispering Pines, where the wind spoke in hushed tones and the stars blinked brightly, lived a young owl named Ori. From hatchling to fledgling, Ori was taught that silence was wisdom,

and that listening was the path to truth. The elders said, 'Stillness brings clarity, and clarity brings peace.'

Ori grew wise in the ways of the grove, but as the seasons turned, Ori had a longing to go beyond the pines. 'There must be more to the world than the whispering wind,' thought the owl, and one evening, spread wings to fly.

Arriving first in the Clattering Canyons, he met owls who hooted in harmony and beat their wings to echoing rhythms. 'Noise is our language,' they said. 'It binds us together.' Ori listened, and though it was different, did not judge.

Next came the Stormlight Savannah, where the skies changed daily and owls danced with the wind. 'Change is our teacher,' they said. 'We learn by moving.' Ori watched, found it unfamiliar, and did not criticise.

Then came the City of Shifting Shadows, where owls vanished and reappeared, blending with the ever-turning world. 'Ambiguity is our strength,' they said. 'We see what others miss.' Ori observed, and though it was unclear, did not fear.

In time, owls from all lands gathered beneath a full moon, hoping to understand one another. With each loudly speaking their own truth, none could be heard – nor could they hear. The canyon owls grew loud, the savannah owls shifted restlessly, and the city owls faded into silence.

In the way of Whispering Pines, Ori had been consciously listening to discern the various messages. Holding up a wing from the centre of the clearing, Ori spoke.

Like the wind of Whispering Pines, the message wafted through the chaos. 'We are shaped by where we are from, and each of us carries

a truth, which is our own note. Together, with balance, direction and well-placed pauses, our notes create harmony.'

The owls, at first startled by this revelation, slowly began to discuss; to reveal and to heed. They shared from the perspective of invitation and listened to understand.

Ori eventually returned to Whispering Pines, imparting the lessons of many lands. With the new information, quietly, the grove underwent a shift. Where once the owls listened to confirm their view, they began to hear what had not been previously considered, thereby deepening their wisdom and widening their horizons.

***

Humans carry the beliefs that form our thinking into every environment we enter and bringing multiple convictions into one space does not naturally invite functionality, let alone harmony. Culture is inherently a living system, moulded by the truths we inherit and those we encounter. In times of change, we often seek clarity by holding tightly to what we know but transformation begins when we loosen that grip.

Research across cultural evolution, organisational psychology and leadership studies shows that sustainable change emerges when we navigate multiple truths and perspectives *in tandem*.[1,2] This capacity is essential for building systems that perform under pressure. For us, the ability to hold multiple perspectives is a cognitive skill stemming from a regulated state; when stress loads the system, attention narrows, resulting in a more reactive and less flexible perspective.

Every person arrives at work carrying their own experiences, pressures and priorities. Our individual concerns generate noise, and

it's embarrassingly naïve to assume that going to work somehow turns that off. When the conditions of work ignore this reality, focus erodes and effort becomes inefficient. If our goal is results and resilience, accepting reality is essential. And in organisations, the extent of that acceptance is evident in the state of employee mental health and psychological safety at work.

Results require focus, and a noisy mind fragments focus. Balanced mental health and a firm sense of psychological safety are therefore foundational conditions for productivity and growth. The World Health Organization (WHO) estimates that depression and anxiety cost the global economy US$1 trillion annually in lost productivity, with 12 billion workdays lost each year. Gallup's *State of the Global Workplace 2024* reports that 44% of employees experience significant daily stress, a predictor of burnout and disengagement.[3]

Research consistently shows that wellbeing initiatives act as powerful performance multipliers. The WHO reports an average return of approximately 4:1 for every unit invested in mental health support, driven primarily by gains in productivity and sustained high-quality work.[4]

Corporate data indicates a similar trend: 95% of organisations that track their Return on Wellness see positive returns, with many achieving 2:1 or higher resulting from improved engagement, stronger retention and more effective teams.[5] [6] The practical effect is faster execution and sustained organisational agility.

What is this book about?

Curiosity is often the starting point for meaningful change, because it creates space to question assumptions and imagine alternatives. If you've picked up this book, you are likely prepared to question whether the ways we've been working still serve the direction we're moving in.

The ideas in this book grew from having curiosity-based conversations with guests of my podcast whose expertise spans organisational change, applied psychology, movement science and more. The introduction of psychosocial legislation in Australia prompted a broader examination of how workplaces might evolve beyond compliance requirements to support wellbeing and resilience as contributors to sustained performance.

The aim became clear: to connect scientific knowledge, cultural awareness, and lived experience in a way that supports both wellbeing and performance. A practical and human-centred approach to achieving optimal workforce outcomes. To that end, this book focuses on the conditions under which people thrive and performance follows, generating a Return on Wellness. Here, let's call it *ROW*.

Imagining a new kind of workplace

This book extends the conversation beyond the individual mindset, examining how organisational structures, systemic barriers, and collaborative practices influence wellbeing and performance at scale.

The idea of a growth mindset has taken root across the globe within the business, government and education sectors. In Australia, it began appearing in primary schools around 2012, encouraging young minds to explore multiple perspectives and expand their sense of possibility. Over time, the principles of the growth mindset made their way into the professional world, influencing how teams approach information, change, and leadership.

While a growth mindset encourages adaptability and personal resilience, its application remains an individual pursuit, detached from the structural conditions that determine progression and reward. The systems and environments we're part of influence, and often constrain, personal development. When the barriers to progress are structural rather than personal, mindset alone is insufficient to achieve resilience.

Through cycles of learning, adapting, and evolving, organisations have built momentum and accumulated new tools, but momentum does not guarantee progress. Are we poised for success? Have we defined what success looks like or how to measure it?

The challenges we face today are complex and interconnected, requiring a shift beyond individual optimisation toward coordinated thinking, shared responsibility, and effective collaboration. The task ahead is to determine what comes next and to articulate a future state we can work toward with clarity and intent. What will our priorities be? And within environments accustomed to constant motion and accumulation, how will we know when we have arrived?

Is this a pivotal moment where the proverbial pause is advisable? Author Stephen R. Covey in *The 7 Habits of Highly Effective People*, along with Tracy Kennedy of Forbes Coaches Council and Peter Ray, long-time biopharma executive, each conclude that even a 10-second pause can shift decision-making from impulsive to deliberate, reducing errors and improving outcomes.

This sounds simple, but in some settings, pausing for 10 seconds can invite interruption, dismissal, or the immediate surfacing of perceived obstacles. In many contemporary workplaces, the normalised pace makes it difficult to pause. Without the pause, we cannot reflect and recalibrate – conditions essential for mental clarity and realising a ROW.

Without clarity, it becomes difficult to sustain direction. Purpose, thoughtful preparation and the capacity to translate insight into action underpin effective performance. Maintaining this capacity requires recognising the human factors that drive it.

Mental clarity is affected by the strength of the conditions supporting both body and mind. Research identifies several factors that influence sustained performance:

- **Physical foundations** – adequate sleep, balanced nutrition and regular movement maintain cognitive sharpness and emotional stability.[7]
- **Psychological safety** – environments where individuals feel safe to share ideas without fear reduce stress and free mental capacity for focus and creativity.[8]
- **Self-concept clarity** – understanding your role and purpose strengthens motivation and reduces mental strain, enabling sustained attention.[9]
- **Organisational clarity** – transparent goals and well-structured processes minimise ambiguity, which otherwise drains mental energy and impairs decision-making.[10]

These elements work together to create conditions where clarity is continuous rather than fleeting, allowing individuals to perform at their best while protecting their wellbeing. Recent evidence supports this connection.

A study in Türkiye found that self-concept clarity enhances intrinsic motivation through psychological empowerment, showing that when individuals understand their identity and role, they experience greater meaning and competence at work.[11] Research from Italy demonstrates that perceived organisational support and clarity improve mental wellbeing and job satisfaction, which in turn drive higher performance.[12]

At scale, the absence of these conditions shows up clearly in the data. Rising global burnout rates reflect what happens when psychological stability is eroded. Balanced cognitive and emotional states are essential to solid results, yet burnout has become a material constraint on that capacity.

Amid ongoing market and organisational volatility, it is the human system that increasingly determines whether organisational goals can be met. How can we use technology and the insights we've gathered to create environments where human beings flourish naturally? How might we encourage a reimagining of how we relate to work, to each other, and to the systems we are part of?

As work continues to change, organisations are increasingly reliant on human capability rather than technical skill alone. A recent conversation with my son, who is in his final year of high school and beginning to think about what to study at university, brought these questions into sharp focus.

Our discussion centred on how best to prepare for a world in which roles and expectations are liable to shift repeatedly. The emphasis was on developing adaptive capability, alongside thinking about the kind of work a person might keep investing in as interests and circumstances evolve. It is no longer 'what do I want to be when I grow up,' but 'how do I want to keep working as the world continues to change'.

The World Economic Forum surveyed employers globally and found that by 2030, 39% of core job skills will have changed.[13] Employers are strongly emphasising a blend of cognitive, emotional and collaborative capabilities, highlighting the importance of interdisciplinary fluency.

Technology is driving which human skills are valued within organisational systems. As repetitive and rule-based tasks are automated, value increasingly sits with human judgement alongside technological capability.

Skills losing value	Skills gaining value
Routine data entry	AI literacy and automation management
Basic customer service (call centres)	Emotional intelligence and empathy
Manual scheduling and admin tasks	Critical thinking and complex problem-solving
Repetitive manufacturing tasks	Creativity and innovation
Basic IT support	Cybersecurity and data privacy expertise
Transactional sales	Strategic communication and influence
Standardised reporting	Analytical thinking and data interpretation
Low-level compliance checking	Adaptability and resilience in dynamic systems

While the next generation has the advantage of a considered approach to the future, living through this transformation as part of the workforce is often exhilarating, exhausting, not to mention expensive. In the last decade, people have navigated constant shifts in workplace structures, a global health crisis and the emergence of a new digital, political, and economic reality.

Across industries and hierarchies, anxiety about the future is rising. The performance tools currently in place are reactive, addressing symptoms only after disruption has taken hold and arriving too late to prevent breakdown.

SYSTEMIC INTERVENTION

Consider the impact if we were to approach human potential in the workplace systemically. The World Economic Forum highlights that workplaces prioritising mental, emotional, and physical wellbeing are more likely to achieve stronger productivity and performance gains.[14] This underscores a broader strategic gap: the lack of integrated approaches that connect human wellbeing to sustainable business outcomes.

Clarity and ability to focus are dependent on the state of the workplace, and wellbeing has a measurable economic impact. OECD research shows that impaired cognitive functioning reduces task effectiveness and increases errors, undermining productivity. Presenteeism and absenteeism contribute additional strain across member countries.[15] These effects reflect diminished capacity rather than a lack of effort.

Targeted, evidence-informed wellbeing strategies address this directly by strengthening clarity and cognitive capacity at a system level. When organisations invest intentionally in human capacity, they create the basis for more consistent performance and greater resilience. OECD data show that the cost of neglecting wellbeing is measurable both in human terms and in the billions of lost economic value. Leaders who invest in supportive conditions are therefore not making a discretionary choice, but securing the conditions for growth and competitive advantage.

Source	Key statistic	Meaning	Leadership implication
OECD Compendium of Productivity Indicators (2024)	Sustained productivity growth depends on effective labour utilisation, human capital quality, and the ability of people to perform consistently over time	Productivity gains are increasingly constrained by human, not technical, limits. Where clarity, capacity, and engagement erode, productivity growth stalls	Healthy, engaged employees are foundational to long-term performance and growth
OECD Promoting Health and Wellbeing at Work (2022)	Workplace well-being programs reduce sickness absence and increase participation, delivering measurable productivity gains across sectors	OECD evidence shows that preventive investment outperforms reactive responses, reducing avoidable disruption before performance deteriorates	Investing in wellbeing lowers costs, improves workforce availability, and strengthens organisational capacity
OECD Mental Health and Work Policy Framework (underpinned by A New Benchmark for Mental Health Systems, 2021)	Mental ill-health drives economic costs of up to 4% of GDP across OECD countries, with more than a third attributable to lost productivity, absenteeism, and reduced workforce participation	At a macro level, this represents a structural loss of productive capacity equivalent to a permanent reduction in economic output, not a marginal cost. Losses recur annually and extend well beyond healthcare into labour markets and organisational performance	Addressing mental health is not discretionary; it is essential for economic resilience, workforce stability, and sustained performance

The evidence increasingly points to the need to rethink how technology can support human wellbeing and productivity. While digital systems are designed to drive efficiency, the opportunity lies in how the time and attention those efficiencies release can be reinvested into clearer thinking and sustained focus.

Research and advisory firm Gartner's recent research shows that human-centric workplaces consistently deliver measurable gains in performance and engagement.[16] This reinforces the importance of treating wellbeing as a core operating principle, rather than an add-on: a foundational condition that enables people to meet the cognitive and interpersonal demands of modern work.

What is stress? Is it burnout?

The human concept of stress has evolved over time.

Hippocrates, around 400 BCE, described health as a balance and harmony of the four humours. Wellbeing was achieved when these elements were in proper proportion and well mixed into a state known as *krasis*.

Epicurus, in around 300 BCE, introduced the idea of *ataraxia*, a state of mental tranquillity, freedom from fear and absence of bodily pain. For him, inner peace was the foundation of a good life.

In 1854, Claude Bernard laid the foundation for modern physiology with his concept of the *milieu intérieur*, or internal environment. He argued that a stable internal environment is essential for the free and independent life of higher organisms. His insight was clear: 'the constancy of the internal environment is the condition for free and independent life.'

Walter Cannon expanded on this in the 1930s with the concept of *homeostasis*. He described it as a self-regulating process that maintains internal equilibrium through coordinated physiological responses. His work shaped the modern understanding of how the body responds to threats and maintains balance, including the fight, flight and freeze responses.

Hans Selye, beginning in 1936 and continuing into the 1950s, introduced the modern concept of stress. He showed that a wide range of stressors – physical, emotional or environmental – could trigger the same biological response. This became known as the General Adaptation Syndrome. It unfolds in three stages: alarm, resistance and exhaustion. As Selye's scientific framework gained traction, the language of the experience of stress began to enter everyday life, reshaping how individuals and societies described emotional and physical strain.

Burnout, fatigue, pressure, anxiety, trauma, tension, hassle, strain, worry: these are all modern terms for *stress*. The casual use of 'I'm stressed' gained traction in the 1950s, alongside the rise in the use of diazepam, trade name Valium, often referred to as mother's little helper thanks to the song of that name by The Rolling Stones.[17]

Under Australian legislation designed to manage psychosocial risks, particularly the *Work Health and Safety (Managing Psychosocial Hazards at Work) Code of Practice 2024*, stress is not classified as an injury.[18] However, it is recognised as a response to psychosocial hazards that can lead to psychological or physical harm when frequent, prolonged or intense.

Stress is a familiar concept in today's work environments. It has been widely studied, frequently discussed, and absorbed into everyday language. Among competing definitions and interpretations, the following definition continues to resonate, particularly in the context of how people experience pressure, pace and expectation at work.

*Psychological and physical strain or tension generated by physical, emotional, social, economic or occupational circumstances, events or experiences that are **difficult** to manage or endure.*[19]

The word *difficult* often describes a challenge; something to be overcome. In many workplaces, competition is used as motivation, creating conditions for chronic stress. This form of stress is persistent, recurring and long-term.

While stress can be a temporary response to pressure, burnout is the result of a more sustained erosion over time. It makes visible a breakdown in the relationship between people and the systems they work within. Burnout often emerges when high demands are paired with low support, when effort goes unrecognised, and when people feel disconnected from purpose or impact.

In many cases, the intensity of work alone is not leading to burnout. The lack of space to recover, review and re-engage is exactly where the key to reducing burnout lies. Understanding burnout requires us to look beyond individual resilience and examine the expectations and conditions of everyday working life.

Contemporary complexities

Workplaces today are a mix of accelerating change, rising expectations and shifting norms. People are expected to be adaptive, emotionally resilient, consistently productive and thoroughly engaged, often without the structures or support to make those expectations reasonable or sustainable. To understand what people are experiencing, we need to look closely at four interconnected dynamics: burnout, fatigue, stress, and resistance to returning to the office post-COVID. Each dynamic indicates a growing tension between how work is designed and how people are expected to show up within it.

> The gap between what work demands and what it enables is where strain accumulates. When expectations rise without the resources or clarity to match, the effects show in behaviour.

Alex faces mounting deadlines with little room to prioritise. Meetings reveal the pressure: speech quickens, interruptions occur and attention drifts to emails. Lunch breaks disappear and late nights become routine. These patterns show stress. Errors increase, collaboration weakens and trust begins to erode.

Jordan's experience highlights the same imbalance. Extended hours without recovery leave Jordan yawning through meetings, missing details and withdrawing from discussion. Fatigue slows decisions and undermines accuracy, creating delays and raising the risk of absence.

Sam's situation has moved beyond strain into burnout. Cynicism colours conversations, collaboration is avoided and unplanned absences mount. When present, Sam speaks with detachment, questioning the point of the work. The impact is clear: morale declines, knowledge is lost and replacement costs rise.

These scenarios show how strain appears in meetings, in tone, and in the quality of work. If we were in a team-building workshop, we would discuss what interventions could close the gap and restore balance. After that workshop we would return to our desks, where the system had not changed.

A systemic review of over 20 studies involving more than 2,600 participants found that habit sustainability is strongly influenced by environmental cues, contextual repetition, and reinforcement through consistent cue-response pairings.[20] When these cues are absent, habits remain fragile and require ongoing, conscious effort – otherwise known as willpower. In other words, without a supportive and stable context, habits are far less likely to become automatic and may fail after initial motivation wanes. The question of intervention is larger than colleague-to-colleague interim measures.

STRESS: A NORMALISED STATE OF DISCONNECTION

Stress is embedded in the language of work. It is expected and often rewarded. But prolonged stress without relief leads to depletion. In many organisations, stress is treated as a sign of commitment. Long hours, constant urgency and reactive decision-making are seen as indicators of dedication. This culture undermines the very outcomes it seeks to produce.

The challenge is to understand the sources of stress and design work in ways that allow for agency. When stress becomes the default state, it signals that something in the system needs to shift.

FATIGUE: THE QUIET EROSION OF CAPACITY

Fatigue builds slowly, eroding energy and diminishing the capacity to engage with work and with others. In workplaces where change is constant and expectations are ambiguous, fatigue becomes a baseline condition: normalised, and at significant cost.

Fatigue affects more than the body. It alters how people think and relate, particularly when work demands constant context-switching, sustained attention and performance without a pause. These effects are amplified by digital overload and the pressure to be always available.

Organisations rarely measure fatigue directly, but its effects are visible in decision quality, pace and how people engage with colleagues and clients.

BURNOUT: WHEN THE SYSTEM ITSELF BEGINS TO FAIL

Burnout is increasingly recognised as a growing workplace-specific condition. The WHO describes it as 'an occupational phenomenon resulting from chronic workplace stress that has not been successfully managed.'[21] It is marked by exhaustion, mental distance or cynicism about one's job, and a decline in professional efficacy. This framing locates burnout in the conditions of work, rather than an individual weakness.

Burnout tends to emerge where sustained effort is required without adequate recovery, recognition or connection to meaningful contribution. While organisational responses often focus on individual coping strategies, the primary drivers sit elsewhere: in how work is structured, value recognised and performance expectations set.

In 2024, the WHO reinforced this 'systems view' through updated guidance on mental health in the workplace, emphasising that 'decent work' supports mental health.[22] Decent work is defined by safety and fair conditions, as well as by predictable structures and reliable livelihoods that support effective daily functioning. These are the conditions that prevent chronic workplace stress from taking hold

In contrast, poor working environments, characterised by excessive workloads, limited autonomy, discrimination and job insecurity, are associated with higher rates of depression and anxiety. Globally, an estimated 12 billion working days are lost each year as a result, at a cost exceeding one trillion US dollars.[23]

For organisations, burnout is therefore a health concern and a material performance and governance issue. Mental health is affected by the systems people work within, and those systems increasingly sit within regulatory and risk frameworks. In Australia, for example, Work Health & Safety (WHS) laws require employers to identify and manage psychosocial risk at work, including excessive job demands and unclear roles. More broadly, addressing burnout means redesigning work conditions to support sustainable engagement, rather than relying on short-term fixes or individual coping strategies.

RETURN TO OFFICE RESISTANCE: A QUESTION OF VALUE, TRUST AND RELEVANCE

The reluctance to return to physical workplaces since the pandemic points to a more fundamental concern regarding trust and relevance. For many people, remote and hybrid arrangements improved their ability to manage their time and direct their energy. Against that experience, mandated returns can feel like reversion.

The resistance is less about location and more about conditions. People want environments that respect time and energy. Organisations that ignore these indicators risk disengagement and attrition, while those that respond have an opportunity to co-create new models of presence and collaboration.

Flexibility is necessary, but insufficient

Flexibility alone won't get you where you want to be.

While hybrid work boosts satisfaction, the core challenge is rebuilding connection, trust and team cohesion in a workplace where physical presence is no longer the norm.

Results from Future Forum's Winter 2022-23 Pulse Survey underscore why more than a geographic shift is critical.[24]

- **Isolation is rising** – desk workers report a declining sense of belonging and weaker ties to colleagues, even in flexible set-ups.
- **Collaboration suffers** – teams without intentional connection strategies experience lower engagement and slower decision-making.

- **Burnout persists** – Future Forum found 42% of workers felt burned out, and while flexibility helps, without cultural and environmental redesign, stress remains high.
- **Culture matters** – workers with flexibility and strong team connection are 57% more likely to say culture improved, proving that flexibility must be paired with deliberate collaboration practices.
- **Leadership gap** – executives often underestimate the need for new norms. As Future Forum notes, 'one size fits nobody.' Transformation means rethinking how teams interact, share context and build trust, which is more nuanced than simple geography.

WHEN DEMANDS OUTPACE RECOVERY

At work, risks to mental health are often described as psychosocial risks. They stem from how work is designed and governed. The risks are inherent in the content and pace of work, the conditions in which it is carried out, and the extent to which people can use and develop their capability.

Common psychosocial risks include sustained overload, limited control over how work is done, unclear expectations, job insecurity, and insufficient organisational support. They are further reinforced by workplace norms that tolerate harmful behaviour or make it difficult to recover from work demands.

In aggregate, these conditions describe environments in which demands consistently outpace recovery opportunities.

Why redesign is unavoidable

Future Forum's findings support that flexibility is an important part of the fuller picture. Hybrid work changes logistics. Whether it supports connection and mental wellbeing depends on how work is intentionally designed.

> Improving performance and sustaining capacity require a model that goes beyond logistics to consider what reinforces human functioning over time.

This is where neuroscience offers guidance. The Healthy Mind Platter™, developed by renowned American psychiatrist Dr. Dan Siegel, MD and colleagues, provides a framework for the mental nutrition individuals and teams need to thrive, complementing flexibility with practices that build focus, creativity and connection.[25]

The Healthy Mind Platter explained

A science-based framework for mental wellbeing, The Healthy Mind Platter is analogous to a balanced diet: just as our bodies need a variety of nutrients, our minds require diverse daily activities to thrive. The model identifies seven essential mental activities that support optimal brain function, emotional regulation and resilience.

1. **Focus time** – concentrating on goal directed tasks strengthens neural connections and builds mastery.
2. **Play time** – engaging in spontaneous, creative activities fosters flexibility and innovation.
3. **Connecting time** – nurturing relationships and connecting with nature activates social and relational circuits.
4. **Physical time** – moving the body enhances brain health, reduces stress and improves mood.

5. **Time in** – reflecting inward through mindfulness or introspection promotes self-awareness and emotional balance.
6. **Down time** – allowing the mind to wander or rest without structured goals rejuvenates mental energy.
7. **Sleep time** – prioritising restorative sleep consolidates memory and supports emotional regulation.

The platter advocates for a holistic approach to mental health, emphasising that wellbeing depends on integrating all these activities into daily life.

Grounded in neuroscience and psychology, the model supports practices that reduce stress, prevent burnout, enhance creativity and strengthen social bonds. It aligns with evidence that mental health and performance improve when individuals experience balance across cognitive, emotional and relational domains.

CONNECT THE DOTS: THE SYSTEM IS SPEAKING

The WHO has acknowledged that civil society must play a role in addressing the burnout crisis. The Healthy Mind Platter illustrates the essential ingredients for mental wellbeing, offering a framework for what the brain needs each day to function well. Research from Future Forum underscores the urgency of taking action to redesign work environments that support these needs.

Addressing burnout cannot rely on individual coping strategies or superficial perks. When organisational structures normalise over-availability and sustained intensity without sufficient recovery, temporary fixes do little to change outcomes. Sustainable progress depends on creating healthy workload design and on norms that value clarity and rest alongside achievement. Responsibility sits with leadership and policy to determine and influence conditions that allow people to meet expectations without sacrificing their health.

What does systemic redesign look like?

Current approaches include workload audits, flexible scheduling and leadership training to recognise early signs of strain. These are important steps, but the next wave of solutions will go further, embedding wellbeing into the architecture of work itself, such as the following.

- **Holistic health investment** – organisations are beginning to treat employee health as a strategic asset rather than a discretionary benefit. McKinsey estimates that prioritising workforce health could unlock up to US$11.7 trillion in global economic value, driven by higher productivity and reduced absenteeism.[26] This means integrating wellbeing into business planning as a core performance driver.
- **Sentient workplace design** – physical environments will evolve to support mental clarity and recovery. WELL-certified spaces, natural light optimisation and sensory design are emerging as standards for workplaces that reduce cognitive load and promote focus.[27] These changes acknowledge that mental health is influenced by both policies and the spaces where work happens.
- **Integrated wellbeing frameworks** – future systems will apply a holistic lens to HR processes, from onboarding to performance reviews, to identify and remove structural drivers of burnout. This includes aligning workload expectations with capacity, embedding recovery periods into project cycles, and ensuring

that recognition systems reward sustainable performance rather than constant overextension.

The challenge is persistent. Integrating wellbeing into daily work is complex. Most people cannot, and do not, manage it alone. Without support and guidance, these practices are often the first to be set aside when time feels limited.

Performance routinely overshadows individual needs, but people achieve more when conditions support focus and recovery. Research now offers clear insight into what sustains capacity over time, showing that human performance, like that of any system, depends on adequate support structures.

Whether in large organisations or smaller, independent settings, when people are well, they do well. Designing workplaces around what supports sustained capacity is therefore not a concession, but a practical way to improve outcomes.

But ... we have an EAP!

This section looks at how people experience workplace systems as they currently exist. Where gender is referenced, it reflects commonly used categories that influence expectations, behaviour and access to support at work. These categories are used here as a practical way to describe observed patterns, not as a statement about identity or how people ought to be.

The way we think about work is shaped by assumptions that no longer reflect lived reality. While employment is essential for survival, it rarely sits at the top of people's priorities. The traditional notion of work–life balance oversimplifies a much more complex reality.

> We need to move beyond the industrial-era model of our current systems and begin designing work cultures based on what we now know about human needs; what supports us and what hinders our performance.

A more useful lens is one of stress mitigation, particularly how allostatic load can be balanced to support effective decision-making. Allostatic load (AL) is a term used in health and psychology to describe the wear and tear on the body and brain that happens when individuals are exposed to chronic stress.

This concept is supported by research by Guidi et al (2021), which defines AL as 'the cumulative burden of chronic stress and life events' involving the interaction of multiple physiological systems that lead to a deterioration in health when overactivated or dysregulated.[28]

In any system, performance depends on balance. In the system of workplace culture, when one person is overloaded, the entire team feels the strain. We cannot function at our best when the load is unevenly distributed.

The same dynamics are at play within the self. To sustain our role in the many teams that rely on us – partners, children, parents, pets, friends, book clubs, even our plants – we must understand and manage our own capacity.

Our World in Data estimates that close to one billion people globally live with a mental health disorder.[29] These include depression, anxiety, bipolar disorder, schizophrenia, eating disorders and substance use disorders; conditions that are the leading causes of disability worldwide.

The WHO estimates that over one billion people worldwide are living with mental health conditions.[30] Global estimates of mental disorder prevalence are derived from systematic reviews and Bayesian meta-regression modelling, which are specifically designed to estimate prevalence even where reporting and diagnostic data are incomplete.[31] Despite this, the global burden of mental illness is widely argued to be underestimated due to classification and measurement limitations, already affecting more than one in eight people worldwide.[32]

If your organisation believes that offering an Employee Assistance Program (EAP) is a sufficient response to burnout, you've missed the boat, and here's why.

1. **Burnout is both a systemic and an individual issue** – talk therapy can be helpful for individuals but it doesn't address the root causes of burnout that often stem from organisational culture, workload design, leadership behaviour and systemic pressures. Treating burnout only at the individual level is like installing better warning lights while leaving the engine unchanged.

2. **Reactive support is not prevention** – by the time someone seeks EAP support, they may already be in the exhaustion phase of burnout. At that point, recovery is slow, costly and often incomplete. What's needed is the proactive design of work environments to prevent burnout from occurring in the first place.

3. **It shifts responsibility away from the organisation** – relying solely on EAPs implies that burnout is a personal failing or weakness, rather than a predictable outcome of unsustainable systems. This can reinforce stigma and discourage early intervention.

4. **It ignores the data** – burnout is widespread and growing. With over a billion people affected by mental health conditions globally, and workplace stress a major contributor, organisations must move upstream and redesign work to support wellbeing. Mitigation is more effective than treatment.

WHY SUPPORT CAN ARRIVE TOO LATE

Support mechanisms such as Employee Assistance Programs are

important, but they are typically engaged once pressure has already exceeded a person's capacity to cope. At that point, stress responses can narrow attention, reduce flexibility, and impair decision-making, rendering it more difficult for people to recognise the relevance of support or engage with it fully. Understanding this progression helps explain why prevention depends on the availability of assistance and on whether environmental conditions allow people the clarity to access that support at the right time.

WINDOW OF TOLERANCE

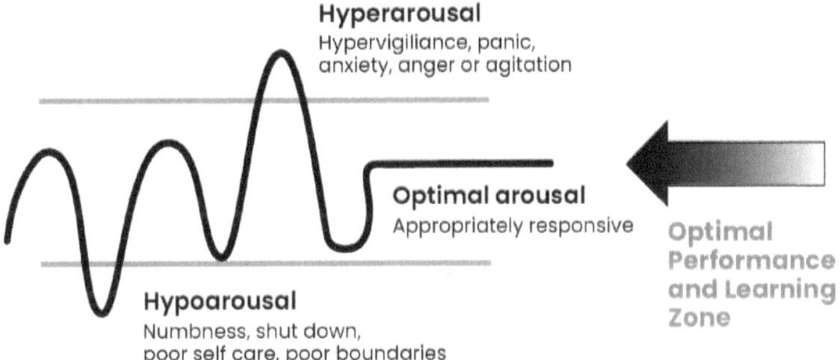

Figure 1 The window of tolerance. A simplified visual representation of the optimal zone of nervous system regulation, illustrating states of hyperarousal and hypo arousal outside this range. Note. Illustration adapted from Lisa Worksheets (n.d.).[33]

As illustrated above, in states of burnout, the nervous system is operating outside what psychiatrist Dan Siegel MD describes as their *Window of Tolerance.*[34] We each have an optimal zone in which we can function well and cope with stress without feeling overwhelmed. Within the optimal zone, daily tasks and life are easier to manage because stress and emotions can be dealt with effectively.

A person experiencing burnout is generally overwhelmed and fatigued, often caught in cycles of apathy, anger or hopelessness. They may feel shame about their state and struggle to make sound decisions. In many cases, they are not even fully aware of how unwell they are.

Do they know your organisation offers EAP services? Do they believe those services are only for crisis situations, for certain levels of seniority, or that using them might stigmatise them? The process for accessing support may be unclear or feel risky. And for many, an ingrained mindset of self-reliance makes them feel like they should be able to handle it alone.

NORMS OF SUCCESS AND THEIR HIDDEN COST

The behaviours associated with the phrase 'traditional masculine norms' are enacted by people across workplaces where such behaviours remain closely equated with success. In many professional environments, these norms - traditionally coded as masculine but not tied to gender - such as emotional restraint, dominance and self-reliance, continue to inform workplace expectations. These norms, often internalised unconsciously, can limit not only wellbeing but also the inclusivity and adaptability of entire organisations. In this context, masculinity is examined as a set of culturally reinforced norms about success and authority, rather than as a gendered trait or identity.

Canadian workplace mental health expert Erin Davis advocates for open dialogue around healthy masculine norms, where leadership is defined not by aggression or control, but by how authority and influence are expressed through emotional intelligence, collaboration and adaptability. These qualities are increasingly recognised as essential for effective leadership and innovation.[35]

Working with depth rather than scale, a 2025 peer-reviewed study published in the *Journal of Men's Health* by researchers from Deakin University explores how masculinity is being understood in the contemporary Australian context as a social expectation rather than a fixed personal identity, with implications extending well beyond the study itself. [36] Drawing on interviews with 39 participants aged 21 to 74 years across gender identities, the study reflects a broad cross-section of adult perspectives.

Within this sample, such norms, including emotional restraint and physical dominance, were frequently described as outdated and overly rigid. Participants instead described masculinity as something that must be acted out or lived up to, rather than something that simply is, alongside a wider definition growing in emphasis on prosocial and human centred traits.

The authors suggest that masculinity in Australia may be at a critical juncture, as emerging interpretations challenge rigid expectations. In doing so, they point toward forms of expression that reduce pressure on individuals to continually perform traditional norms and support healthier workplace cultures.

UK-based organisation Voicebox CIC emphasises that outdated masculine ideals, such as emotional suppression and the need to constantly appear strong, can contribute to burnout, mental health challenges and reduced engagement at work. Through its youth-focused programs, particularly with boys and young men, Voicebox highlights how promoting healthy masculinity supports individual wellbeing, contributing to healthier cultures over time. They recommend training in emotional resilience, inclusive leadership and mental health awareness as key strategies for change.[37]

THE ORGANISATIONAL IMPACT OF THESE NORMS

While rethinking masculinity opens space for healthier, more adaptive workplace cultures, it also brings into focus how organisational systems allocate opportunity, visibility and risk. In many organisations, success continues to be defined through a limited set of behaviours associated with authority and achievement. Those whose ways of working fall outside this pattern face greater constraint, interruption or scrutiny. Examining these dynamics helps explain how workplace cultures restrict talent, leadership capacity and organisational effectiveness.

In practice, leadership potential is often assessed through tightly bounded and internally contradictory expectations. Research consistently identifies structural barriers for people whose behaviour does not align with dominant success norms. These effects are most visible for women, but also by men and LGBTQ+ individuals. Gender bias, entrenched in stereotypes and the ongoing influence of the glass ceiling continue to restrict access to senior roles, even where qualifications and performance are comparable.[38]

Leadership assessment in many organisations still relies on constrained interpretations of authority and emotional expression. Individuals who do not conform precisely to these expectations are more likely to encounter penalty or stalled progression. This pattern is most consistently observed among women, who face well-documented double binds.[39] Assertive behaviour may be interpreted as abrasive, while relational or empathetic approaches are read as a lack of authority. These dynamics are further reflected in the glass cliff phenomenon, in which women are disproportionately appointed to senior roles during periods of instability, increasing risk exposure and the likelihood of blame should outcomes falter.

Where success continues to be defined by uninterrupted availability and linear advancement, career interruptions carry disproportionate cost. Responsibilities related to caregiving, health, or injury often collide with these expectations, creating sustained tension between professional ambition and social roles. The organisational consequences extend beyond individual experience, contributing to chronic stress, stalled progression, and the erosion of workforce continuity, institutional knowledge, and long-term capability.[40]

Within this context, the motherhood penalty represents a well-documented expression of how interruption is penalised within promotion and pay systems, with long-term financial consequences, including reduced retirement security. Many organisational cultures still lack inclusive policies, visible role models and structured mentorship pathways, limiting access to the networks and sponsorships that support advancement.[41]

These effects intensify where misalignment with dominant success norms compounds. Individuals whose identities, circumstances or ways of working fall outside those norms encounter layered barriers across evaluation, progression and access to support.[42] [43]

It can be argued that those most affected by these dynamics are not accessing EAP services. When leaders and employees alike lack timely support, the effects show up in cohesive performance and decision quality across teams. One question is how to reach those who would benefit most from support in ways that feel relevant and safe. Another is why not design for success?

DOES HAVING AN EAP FIX IT?

Offering an EAP may meet a policy requirement, but the investment often goes unused, rendering the spend ineffective and, therefore, a loss. It does not address the underlying causes:

- a lack of proactive risk management
- limited compliance with psychosocial safety guidelines and/ or obligations
- missed opportunities to unlock the full potential of your workforce.

For some, talk therapy feels uncomfortable or impractical. Concerns about confidentiality or the impact on their career often prevent people from engaging with talk therapy. Deliberately addressing the conditions of work reduces the likelihood that strain escalates to the point where reactive support is required.

Time well spent

Time in the workday is often fragmented across meetings, digital distractions and demands that require immediate response. Without structure, flexibility can devolve into dispersed attention.

A meta-analysis of 339 studies across 73 countries found that employee wellbeing is consistently and positively correlated with organisational performance, particularly in areas such as customer satisfaction and staff retention.[44]

> While technology offers tools to support focus and reduce repetitive tasks, under-investment and partial implementation often limit their effectiveness in practice.

With rhythm, coherence is restored

Rhythm refers to the intentional structuring of time to support sustainable focus, energy and engagement. In practice, rhythm is established by how work accounts for energy cycles, cognitive load and relational demands, rather than by scheduling alone. A systematic review of sustainable human resource management practices confirms that wellbeing is enhanced when organisations design work with long-term human sustainability in mind.[45]

Mindfulness contributes to this rhythm. Evidence from organisational case studies shows that mindfulness practices improve psychological capital, emotional intelligence and engagement at individual, team and organisational levels.[46] These practices support clearer thinking, stronger judgement and more resilient performance.

Energy management also plays a critical role. A 2024 study published in the Asia Pacific Journal of Management found that relational energy – the psychological resource derived from positive interpersonal interactions – is a key mechanism linking leadership practices to improved performance and life balance. The study emphasised that relational energy can be cultivated through leadership behaviours and social contagion, enhancing motivation and goal attainment.[47] These findings suggest that rhythm is best understood as a strategic design choice rather than a complementary feature.

THE CASE OF UNILEVER

Unilever's long-term strategy, implemented using its Sustainable Living Plan (USLP), prioritises enduring value over short-term gains. [48] This approach integrates sustainability, innovation and employee wellbeing into core business operations.

- Unilever's adaptive organisational practices, which include mental health initiatives, flexible work design and conscious leadership, have contributed to high employee engagement and organisational resilience.[49]

- The company's commitment to sustainability is a source of competitive advantage, particularly in emerging markets where social and environmental challenges are most acute.

Critically, Unilever's strategy is an example of a shift away from quarterly earnings pressure towards a more values-driven model. This has enabled the company to maintain brand strength, reduce its environmental impact and avoid reputational risks commonly associated with toxic workplace cultures.[50] The evidence suggests that embedding sustainability and wellbeing into strategic planning supports both ethical leadership and long-term performance. For a growing segment of the workforce, particularly younger employees, this alignment between organisational values and everyday practice is not incidental but a key factor in attraction, engagement and retention.

*　*　*

Organisations that translate values into the design of everyday work, such as treating time for reflection as essential rather than optional, see measurable results. These include improvements in wellbeing and performance, alongside reduced incidence of burnout and related absenteeism or workers' compensation claims. Embedding reflection into the rhythm of work, forms healthier cultures that support sound contribution while strengthening longer-term business outcomes.

This approach focuses on preventing strain through design, rather than responding once capacity has already been exceeded.

Movement: A foundation for performance

Over time, our understanding of human movement has undergone a significant transformation. Initially a physical necessity for survival, movement has come to be recognised as foundational to resilience and human performance.

In ancient cultures, movement was embedded in ritual, identity and social cohesion. The athleticism of the Greek Olympians and the disciplined forms of Eastern martial arts share a reverence for physical mastery as a means of cultivating character and harmony.

Writing around 350 BCE, Aristotle described movement as the actualisation of potential. He viewed voluntary motion as a defining feature of life and agency, a perspective that continues to inform contemporary approaches to leadership and personal development.[51]

During the Renaissance, Leonardo da Vinci's anatomical studies revealed a growing fascination with biomechanics and symmetry. His work contributed to a more precise understanding of the human body in motion and laid the groundwork for the scientific study of performance.[52]

In the 17th century, René Descartes introduced a mechanistic view of the body, comparing it to a machine governed by physical laws. This framework influenced early models of motor control and reflex, which continue to influence modern ergonomics and safety protocols.[53]

By the 19th century, advances in neurology and physiology, including the distinction between sensory and motor nerves, began to explain how movement is coordinated by the brain. Movement was increasingly understood as a product of neural communication rather than isolated muscular effort.[54]

In the 20th century, Nikolai Bernstein challenged static models of motor control by demonstrating that movement is dynamic and context-dependent. His work emphasised adaptability and coordination, principles that are now central to agile and responsive work environments.[55]

More recently, movement has been recognised as a regulator of mental health and cognitive function. Practices such as yoga, tai chi and functional movement training have shown that physical activity can reduce stress, enhance executive functioning and support emotional regulation.[56] In contemporary professional settings, intentional movement is used as a strategic tool for wellbeing and performance and is designed into the rhythm of work.[57]

Microbreaks, walking meetings and somatic practices are used to regulate stress, restore cognitive capacity and sustain productivity. Research shows that microbreaks of just a few minutes can reduce fatigue and improve vigour, and companies that embed these practices report measurable gains in engagement and accuracy.

Google encourages walking meetings to stimulate creative thinking, while Salesforce integrates mindful movement sessions into its wellbeing programs.[58] [59] Microsoft promotes the use of active workstations and regular posture changes to help reduce the effects of prolonged static postures.[60] These interventions reveal a growing understanding that movement supports presence, focus and sustainable performance when integrated into organisational systems rather than left to individual willpower.

What organisations are starting to examine is whether learning and adaptation depend as much on physiology as they do on motivation.

Mindful movement and cognitive readiness

Stress, fatigue and cognitive overload impair neuroplasticity, which enables learning and behavioural change. Conversely, practices that regulate the nervous system and engage attentional networks prime the brain for flexibility and retention.

A randomized intervention study published in *Frontiers in Aging Neuroscience* found that a 12 week mindful movement program (Tai Chi) significantly improved working memory performance and increased activation in executive control regions of the brain.[61]

Similarly, a 2024 systematic review in *Biomedicines* reported that mindfulness practices increase cortical thickness and improve connectivity in regions associated with learning and emotional regulation.[62] When movement is integrated, these effects are amplified through sensory engagement and embodied awareness.[63]

The timing of learning interventions is critical for their absorption. Evidence suggests that the period following mindful movement is an optimal window for introducing complex information or collaborative problem-solving. By scheduling training sessions or strategic discussions immediately after short, movement-based mindfulness breaks, organisations can leverage this heightened readiness to improve retention and creative engagement. This approach aligns physiological readiness with cognitive demands and positions wellbeing as a performance strategy.

Companies experimenting with movement-based interventions report measurable benefits. Programs that integrate mindful walking or breath-led stretching before workshops have shown improvements in participants' focus and ability to generate ideas.[64] These findings point to a larger implication: human capacity is not infinitely adaptable, and how work is designed determines whether that capacity is expanded or depleted.

From load to flow:
Rethinking organisational design

Modern organisations already operate with a clear set of assumptions: time is scarce, performance is paramount, and responsiveness is rewarded. What is less often acknowledged is that these assumptions translate directly into physiological load. When work is designed around sustained cognitive demand, constant availability and limited recovery, load accumulates regardless of individual capability or intent.

Movement, recovery, and social connection are widely recognised as supporting human functioning, with well-established physiological benefits, yet in workplace settings, these practices are offered alongside work rather than as conditions embedded within it.[65,66,67,68]

Load is a design outcome, not a personal failing

Allostatic load provides a useful lens for understanding this dynamic. Clinical research identifies allostatic load as a marker of cumulative dysregulation across cardiovascular, endocrine, immune and neurological systems. [69,70,71,72] When demands remain high without sufficient opportunities for regulation and recovery, imbalance becomes normalised rather than exceptional.

Organisational routines play a decisive role here. When cadence-based supports such as coaching, guided check-ins and reflective conversations are embedded within daily work, they help stabilise stress responses and build adaptive capacity over time. Clinical programs that address multiple physiological systems show measurable reductions in allostatic load within weeks, alongside improvements in cardiovascular risk, stronger immune function, improved metabolic regulation, better sleep, reduced anxiety and depression, and sharper cognitive function.[73][74]

Energy, not time, is the limiting factor

Design choices that ignore this reality carry consequences. Work organised around uninterrupted output and continuous responsiveness leaves little space for physiological regulation, increasing burnout risk.

Ultimately, energy – not time – is the primary constraint on high-intensity work. Structures that draw down human capacity faster than it can be restored do not merely affect wellbeing; they undermine judgement, engagement and participation, weakening the very performance they are intended to optimise.

From load reduction to flow capacity

When organisational design aligns more closely with the body's natural rhythms and the brain's need for recovery, work is experienced differently. Removing the expectation of constant real-time response and enabling focused, uninterrupted activity reduces stress and supports sustained effort.

Flow provides a useful way of understanding what becomes possible under these conditions. As described by psychologist Mihaly Csikszentmihalyi, flow is a state of deep engagement characterised by immersion, focused attention and a sense of effortlessness during task engagement.[75] In professional environments, access to flow supports creativity, intrinsic motivation and high-quality performance.

Physiologically, flow depends on the coordinated regulation of multiple systems. [76] Vagal tone supports calm alertness and attentional control, while chronic activation of the hypothalamic-pituitary-adrenal axis elevates cortisol, impairing memory, decision-making and emotional regulation. [77 78 79 80] Recovery practices that activate parasympathetic pathways help restore balance across these systems, enabling the conditions required for flow to emerge.[81]

For neurodivergent individuals, unpredictability and sensory overload can amplify stress responses, making access to flow less reliable. Inclusive and intentional design strategies that reduce these triggers are therefore not optional additions, but prerequisites for equitable participation. [82 83]

Flow as organisational capacity

> Flow is not a finite resource allocated to a few high performers.
> It is a dynamic state that becomes more, or less, accessible
> depending on environmental conditions.

Organisations that embed regulation and recovery into daily rhythms create cultures in which flow can occur during the workday rather than being reserved for exceptional moments.

Practices such as mindfulness and movement are particularly effective in cultivating these conditions. Mindfulness enhances attentional control and emotional regulation, while movement engages sensorimotor networks that support embodied awareness and balance the nervous system. When integrated through breath-led movement, mindful walking or flow-based training protocols, these practices establish the physiological coherence required for sustained engagement.

Built in, not bolted on

Compressing these practices into personal time does not produce the same effect. The physiological reset required for sustained performance must occur during periods of demand. When participation is collective and practices are embedded into organisational routines, the environment normalises and supports these behaviours, reducing reliance on individual willpower.

As a result, focus, autonomy and recovery are intentionally designed into work allowing flow to become repeatable and scalable rather than exceptional.[84]

Learning, adaptability and readiness

The ability to learn and adapt depends on both motivation and physiological state. While motivation influences learning outcomes, physiological state plays a more decisive role in whether learning and adaptation are possible in the first place. Stress, fatigue and cognitive overload impair neuroplasticity, while practices that regulate the nervous system prime the brain for flexibility and retention.

Evidence from neuroscience shows that mindfulness-based movement improves working memory, attentional control and connectivity in regions associated with learning and emotional regulation.[85] The period following such practices represents an optimal window for complex learning, problem-solving and collaboration, positioning wellbeing not as an add-on but as a performance strategy.

From organisational design to cultural responsibility

This shift toward structurally embedded wellbeing is increasingly recognised at a global policy level. The WHO's *Comprehensive Mental Health Action Plan 2013 to 2030* calls for a coordinated action across governments, employers, academic institutions and civil society to create environments that prevent harm and promote wellbeing.[86] The framework reinforces that mental health is not an individual burden, but a shared design responsibility.

Balancing the load: A cultural imperative

Balancing the load has therefore evolved from a logistical concern to a strategic, compliance and cultural priority. Organisations that thrive embed workload awareness into their cultures, supported by open communication and shared accountability for capacity.

Atlassian has long been recognised for its emphasis on transparency and psychological safety, encouraging teams to speak openly about workload and challenges.[87][88] As the organisation evolved, however, changes to performance systems, including the introduction of stack-ranking, raised concerns about increased competition and its potential impact on morale. This illustrates how shifts in organisational design can quietly test even strong cultural foundations.[89]

When teams can articulate their constraints and leaders respond early, pressure is managed before it escalates. Where this transparency erodes, morale becomes fragile. As seen in contexts such as mergers, digital transformation and infrastructure upgrades, morale shapes how initiatives are received, how change takes root and how value is ultimately created. [90] [91]

Load is dynamic, responding to shifting priorities and pressure points. When demands rise without adjustment, engagement falters and execution suffers. Organisations that take visible, inclusive steps to address burnout demonstrate alignment between values and practice, strengthening morale, resilience and long-term performance.

Moving beyond intention

Evidence is mounting that the way work is organised today is not sustainable. Rising burnout rates, alongside increasing regulatory attention to psychosocial safety, highlight that many workplace environments are misaligned with human capacity.

Throughout this book, evidence has shown what enables the human system to function and perform at its best. When these conditions are present, individuals can regulate and sustain performance over time. The next step is translating this understanding into operational and regulatory practice.

Despite this growing body of evidence, organisational investment has largely favoured systems and technology, with comparatively little focus on the human judgement required to navigate complexity. Human judgement converts information into insight. It enables leaders to interpret context, weigh ethical and emotional priorities, and anticipate behavioural and sentiment-driven risk. These capabilities cannot be automated.[92] Strengthening them equips teams to act decisively and responsibly in complex environments.

> To unlock this potential, workplaces must evolve beyond transactional efficiency and become ecosystems that support mind–body synchronisation, where cognitive performance is sustained by physiological rhythms, not depleted by constant demand.

Optimal brain function depends on rhythms that allow recovery, focus and integration. When time is structured to sustain these rhythms, people maintain clarity, manage complexity and apply insight to high-stakes decisions. This is increasingly critical as digital overload, operational pressure and decision velocity intensify.

From insight to implementation

The future of work depends on how leaders turn intention into environments that make certain outcomes more likely.

In practice, this requires embedding recovery and focus directly into the rhythm of work, not around it. Effective organisations do this by designing for:

- Structured focus blocks that reduce fragmentation
- Micro-recovery breaks that restore cognitive capacity
- Meeting formats that prioritise clarity and energy management
- Workload transparency tools that surface hidden overload
- Physical spaces that support movement restoration and collaboration

These design choices align wellbeing with execution rather than positioning it as a discretionary initiative.

Why measurement matters

Today, garnering support to embed wellbeing into organisational strategy requires evidence of its efficacy. Gym memberships and the EAP spend are weak measures in this area, which can lead to hesitance from employers to engage with approaches they misperceive as discretionary rather than demonstrably effective. This requires treating wellbeing as a core measure of organisational success, tracked with the same rigour as financial metrics.

EMPLOYEE WELLBEING MEASUREMENT IN PRACTICE

Employee wellbeing is multidimensional, encompassing physical health, mental resilience, social connection, financial security and career satisfaction.

Gallup conceptualises wellbeing across five interrelated elements: career, social, financial, physical and community wellbeing.[93]

Effective measurement combines:

- Quantitative indicators (e.g. engagement, turnover, workload)
- Qualitative insight (e.g. pulse surveys, open-text feedback)

Key metrics organisations can track

- **Engagement and satisfaction**
  Pulse surveys and eNPS (Employee Net Promoter Score) indicate emotional commitment and experience.
- **Workload balance**
  Overtime, capacity distribution and peak-load indicators signal burnout risk.
- **Participation in wellbeing initiatives**
  Uptake reflects trust, relevance and accessibility.

- **Retention and turnover trends**
  Voluntary attrition correlates strongly with wellbeing culture.
- **Mental health and stress indicators**
  Anonymous surveys utilisation patterns highlight intervention needs.

Viewed together, these provide early signals of where capacity is being supported or strained.

MEASUREMENT AS A VALUE-CREATION LOOP

Tracking is most effective when measurement operates as a continuous loop, moving from experience to insight, informing adjustment and improving experience over time.

Within a ROW framework, value is created when wellbeing insight informs work design changes that improve capacity, decision quality and sustained performance.

Organisations typically triangulate three evidence layers:
- Perception data (what people report)
- Behavioural data (absence, turnover, workload, participation)
- Operational context (restructures, peak periods, major initiatives)

Insight emerges from alignment across these layers not from any single metric.

How to track the subjective, without intrusion

Psychological safety, trust and sentiment are subjective, yet measurable through patterns observed over time.

Effective practice uses short, repeated pulse items focused on the system rather than the individual. Questions assess whether work enables sustainable performance, not whether people are coping.

Example focus areas
- Psychological safety: speaking up, asking for help, admitting mistakes
- Trust: fairness, transparency, follow-through
- Sentiment: manageability, energy, pace of change

The value of these measures lies in movement over time, variation between teams, and alignment with workload and retention data.

Shifts in safety or trust typically precede disengagement, burnout or attrition, making them early-warning indicators.

What enables honest participation

Participation patterns are informative. Neutral or mid-scale responses indicate how safe it feels to provide feedback. These patterns point to system-level risk, not individual reluctance.

Visible response is critical. When feedback leads to tangible changes participation strengthens and measurement itself becomes part of the intervention.

What and when to measure

Effective pulse measurement is intentionally light touch, consistent and comparable over time, with a clear link to action. Its value lies in trend lines that show whether capacity is being built or eroded as work conditions change.

Sample pulse questions

Psychological safety

- I feel safe to speak up or raise concerns
- Mistakes are treated as learning opportunities
- I can ask for help when work becomes unmanageable

Trust

- Leaders follow through on commitments
- Decisions affecting my role are fair and transparent
- My team acts with integrity under pressure

Sentiment

- My work feels manageable and sustainable
- I have the energy and focus to do my best work
- The pace of change currently feels manageable/challenging/ overwhelming

One optional open-text prompt:

- What is currently helping or hindering your ability to do your best work?

How enterprises maximise insight

Enterprises maximise insight when measurement practices are consistent over time, building familiarity and psychological safety rather than reactivity. Respecting anonymity thresholds reinforces trust, while interpreting results alongside workload, change activity and operational pressures prevents responses from being read in isolation. Insight is strengthened when organisations communicate clearly what will change, and what will not, as a result of feedback.

Within a ROW framework, pulse data functions as an early-warning and optimisation system, enabling leaders to detect emerging strain and adjust conditions before cost escalates.

MEASUREMENT AS A CONTRIBUTOR TO RETURN

Gallup reports that companies in the top quartile of employee engagement, an indicator closely tied to wellbeing, achieve 18% higher productivity and 23% greater profitability than those in the bottom quartile.

Modern organisations increasingly integrate wellbeing indicators into operational dashboards alongside KPIs, making the Return on Wellness visible and actionable.[94]

SAP reports a 3:1 return on investment from wellbeing initiatives, driven by engagement, productivity and retention gains.[95] Similar performance improvements are reported by Salesforce, where wellbeing insight is embedded into daily work rhythms.[96]

Research from the University of Oxford shows that higher employee wellbeing is associated with stronger profitability and firm value, with a one-point increase in happiness linked to up to 1.2 percentage points in return on assets.[97]

* * *

Measurement is commonly used to assess performance after the fact. Its greater value lies in making strain and risk visible early, while adjustment is still possible. Treated as a continuous feedback system, wellbeing data informs how work is designed, how pressure is managed and how decisions are made.

This visibility is a prerequisite for responsible implementation. The sections that follow focus on how organisations translate insight into action, designing systems that protect people from harm while enabling performance and, ultimately, profit.

Trauma-informed implementation

Cultural transformation is often considered a structural challenge, yet its success depends on how people experience the change process. As illustrated in the fable that opens this book, employees bring into the workplace ways of thinking, responding and relating that reflect the lives they have lived beyond work. These experiences influence how individuals interpret uncertainty and assess risk. When change initiatives overlook this complexity, the interpersonal risk of speaking up can increase, and the workplace can feel unsafe or overwhelming during periods of transition.

Trauma-informed practice offers a framework for implementing change with care, focusing on the conditions that allow people to stay engaged while uncertainty is high. This aligns closely with research on psychological safety, defined as a work environment where people believe that candid contribution is expected and possible, especially when organisations are navigating change and complexity. Edmondson and Bransby highlight psychological safety as a reduction in interpersonal risk that enables learning in dynamic environments.[98]

FIVE CORE PRINCIPLES FOR TRAUMA-INFORMED CHANGE

- **Safety** – create predictable processes, clear communication and environments that minimise unnecessary stress.
- **Trust and transparency** – communicate decisions openly and consistently to reduce uncertainty and build confidence during periods of change.
- **Choice** – provide opportunities for input and flexibility to support a sense of control during change.
- **Collaboration** – involve employees as partners in developing change, distributing ownership and strengthening relationships
- **Empowerment** – recognise individual strengths and create conditions that support growth and active participation.

These principles are echoed in the WHO's psychosocial support frameworks and in organisational models emphasising safety, trust and empowerment as foundations for sustainable transformation.[99] In ROW terms, trauma-informed change protects the conditions through which safety and performance reinforce one another.

WHERE SAFETY AND PERFORMANCE MEET

Creating a workplace where flow can emerge goes beyond introducing new routines or redesigning schedules, requiring a shift in patterns of behaviour, expectations and relationships. These changes can feel disruptive if not handled carefully. As people with diverse experiences enter this process, past stress or adversity may amplify feelings of uncertainty for some. Without a trauma-informed approach, initiatives intended to enhance wellbeing and performance risk triggering anxiety or resistance.

Effective implementation therefore depends on practitioners guiding these programs being equipped to create psychological safety while introducing new practices such as mindful movement, recovery breaks and autonomy-focused workflows. Trauma-informed expertise ensures that the implementation respects individual thresholds for change, communicates clearly and provides choice wherever possible. This includes pacing the rollout of interventions, offering predictable structures, and preparing leaders to recognise signs of strain and respond in ways that support stability and engagement.

Embedding the five trauma-informed principles of safety, trust, choice, collaboration and empowerment into the delivery of flow-inducing programs protects the workforce during transition. Following this framework improves engagement as employees understand the purpose of change and feel confident knowing how it will affect them. Safe, transparent change creates conditions where new habits take root and grow. In this way, trauma-informed practice becomes a critical enabler of the cultural transformation outlined in this book.

Safe flow considerations

1. Communicate with clarity

- Share the purpose and benefits of the program in simple, accessible language.
- Provide timelines and expectations early to help people feel informed and prepared.

2. Pace change thoughtfully

- Introduce new practices gradually, starting with small steps, such as short mindful movement breaks.

- Allow time for feedback and adjustment before moving to the next stage.

3. Offer choice and flexibility

- Provide options for how employees engage with new practices, e.g. different movement or mindfulness activities.
- Respect individual preferences and offer alternatives.

4. Build supportive structures

- Create spaces for feedback and discussion where employees feel heard.
- Ensure access to wellbeing resources and guidance for those who want extra support.

Designing for human potential *and* profit

The future is the result of the choices made today. Observation, research and legislation show that the current state of our world of work is unsustainable because it is making people unwell. This book has explored the science and practice of creating environments where wellbeing and performance reinforce one another. Resilience grows through consistent habits, and clarity emerges when human capacity is supported through design. Flow, that state of zeroed-in engagement where the magic happens, can be cultivated deliberately.

Organisations that integrate wellbeing into their core strategy are already seeing measurable impact. SAP's investment in wellbeing delivers a clear return.[100] Salesforce demonstrates how cultures of psychological safety support growth.[101] Research from the University of Oxford reinforces the financial case, showing that improvements in employee wellbeing correlate with higher profitability and firm value.[102]

Workplaces are living systems, as are the humans within them. Both function best when work supports balance and makes space for attention as part of everyday practice. Designing environments that recognise human complexity and how people thrive is therefore not optional. It enables collective progress.

Energy sustains performance. How work is designed determines whether that energy is preserved or consumed. When organisations reinvest time and attention into conditions that support human capacity, clarity and effectiveness follow. This is the logic that underpins a Return on Wellness.

Awareness of psychosocial risk and mental health at work is necessary, but insufficient. Change occurs only when understanding is translated into sustained shifts in how work happens. When work is designed to support human capacity, wellbeing and results no longer compete. They reinforce one another.

The outcome follows the design.

Acknowledgements

To everyone whose encouragement played a part in bringing this book together, thank you. Your support was invaluable.

Special shout-outs to J.B. & S.B. for being such cool people to live with, and for their unwavering belief in me.

In gratitude to R.T. for your untiring support, patience and clear advice.

Appreciation for S.H., whose knowledgeable and sage perspective helped sharpen my thinking.

A.M., fabulous friend of challenging and witty repartee, thanks for the comment that sparked this missive.

Un grand merci to Ladybug, who sat near me for many hours during the writing of this book.

In love and gratitude for the privilege of knowing amazing people who helped create the space and mindset required to produce this.

And to you, Readers, thank you for staying with me. My fondness for Aesop's fable found its way into these pages in the form of one I wrote myself; I trust it earned its place. The rest is now yours.

About the author

Elizabeth Blackley is the founder of NeoConnections, bringing the pause into organisations seeking clarity, connection and better ways of working. She is also the host of *eli b. talkin'*, an interview-based podcast that explores what kind of future we want and what it will take to get there.

For over twenty years, Elizabeth has helped organisations navigate change in ways that mitigate stress, unlock potential and recognise their employees as humans first, resources second. Drawing on her experience in organisational change and systems thinking across Australia and the United States, she brings a global perspective to structuring work environments and practices that work for those at all levels of an organisation. In doing so, she helps companies leverage human energy and adaptability for greater creativity and stronger results. Her work champions environments where people thrive and performance follows.

Based in Melbourne, Elizabeth shares her life with two teens and Ladybug – the cat who helps them remember to stay curious.

About NeoConnections

For those grappling with this challenge, structured approaches can help leaders and teams build these capabilities in a sustained way. NeoConnections™ has developed *Implement the Pause™*, an approach that supports organisations to balance mental health, manage psychosocial risk, and embed durable changes into workplace rhythms. For readers seeking to move from insight to implementation, this can be a starting point.

neoconnections.com.au

Endnotes

[1] Brooks, J. S., Waring, T. M., Borgerhoff Mulder, M., & Richerson, P. J. (2018). Applying cultural evolution to sustainability challenges: An introduction to the special issue. *Sustainability Science, 13*(1), 1–8.
https://doi.org/10.1007/s11625-017-0516-3

[2] Smith, W. K., & Lewis, M. W. (2011). Toward a theory of paradox: A dynamic equilibrium model of organizing. *Academy of Management Review, 36*(2), 381–403.
https://doi.org/10.5465/amr.2011.59330958

[3] Gallup. (2024). *State of the global workplace report.*
https://healthyworkcompany.com/wp-content/uploads/2024/08/state-of-the-global-workplace-2024-key-insights.pdf

[4] World Health Organization. (2024, September 2). *Mental health at work.*
https://www.who.int/news-room/fact-sheets/detail/mental-health-at-work

[5] Brooks et al. (2018), *Applying cultural evolution.*

[6] Smith, W. K., & Lewis, M. W. (2011). Toward a theory of paradox.

[7] Garrett, J., Chak, C., Bullock, T., & Giesbrecht, B. (2024). A systematic review and Bayesian meta-analysis provide evidence for an effect of acute physical activity on cognition in young adults. *Communications Psychology, 2,* Article 82.
https://doi.org/10.1038/s44271-024-00124-2

[8] Capezio, A., Barends, E., Rousseau, D., & Wietrak, E. (2023). *Psychological safety: An evidence review (Scientific summary).* Chartered Institute of Personnel and Development.
https://www.cipd.org/globalassets/media/knowledge/knowledge-hub/evidence-reviews/2024-pdfs/8550-psychological-safety-scientific-summary.pdf

[9] Özcan, E., & Yıldırım, M. (2025). Self-concept clarity and intrinsic motivation: The mediating role of psychological empowerment. *Turkish Journal of Psychology, 40*(1), 23–38.

10   Zettna, N., Yam, C., Kunzelmann, A., Forner, V. W., Dey, S., Askovic, M., Johnson, A., Nguyen, H., Jolly, A., & Parker, S. K. (2025). Crystal clear: How leaders and coworkers together shape role clarity and wellbeing for employees in social care. *Human Resource Management, 64*, 5–20.
https://doi.org/10.1002/hrm.22245

11   Özcan, E., & Yildirim, M. (2025).

12   Capezio, A., et al (2023). *Psychological safety*

13   World Economic Forum. (2025). *The future of jobs report 2025.*
https://www.weforum.org/publications/the-future-of-jobs-report-2025/digest

14   World Economic Forum. (2024). *Wellbeing and mental health.*
https://www.weforum.org/stories/wellbeing-and-mental-health

15   Organisation for Economic Co-operation and Development. (2021). *OECD compendium of productivity indicators 2021*. OECD Publishing

16   Gartner. (2025, January 8). *Gartner identifies top nine workplace predictions for CHROs in 2025.*
https://www.gartner.com/en/newsroom/press-releases/2025-01-08-gartner-identifies-top-nine-workplace-predictions-for-chros-in-2025

17   Atkins, H. (2022). *Mother's little helper. The history of Valium.* History Hit.
https://www.historyhit.com/mothers-little-helper-the-history-of-valium

18   Safe Work Australia. (2024). *Work Health and Safety (Managing Psychosocial Hazards at Work) Code of Practice 2024.*
https://www.legislation.gov.au/F2024L01380/latest/text

19   Colman, A. M. (2015). *A dictionary of psychology (4th ed)*. Oxford University Press.
https://www.oxfordreference.com/display/10.1093/acref/9780199657681.001.0001/acref-9780199657681-e-8038

20   Singh, B., Murphy, A., Maher, C., & Smith, A. E. (2024). *Time to form a habit: A systematic review and meta-analysis of health behaviour habit formation and its determinants.* Healthcare, 12(23), 2488.
https://doi.org/10.3390/healthcare12232488

21   World Health Organization. (2019). *Burn-out an "occupational phenomenon": International Classification of Diseases (11th rev.).*
https://www.who.int/standards/classifications/frequently-asked-questions/burn-out-an-occupational-phenomenon

22   World Health Organization. (2024). *Mental health at work* (Fact sheet).
https://www.who.int/news-room/fact-sheets/detail/mental-health-at-work

23   World Health Organization & International Labour Organisation. (2022). *Mental health at work: Policy brief.* World Health Organization.
https://www.who.int/publications/i/item/9789240057944

24   Future Forum. (2023). *Future Forum Pulse report: Winter 2022–2023—Amid spiking burnout, workplace flexibility fuels company culture and productivity.*
https://futureforum.com/wp-content/uploads/2023/02/Future-Forum-Pulse-Report-Winter-2022-2023.pdf

25   Rock, D., Siegel, D. J., Poelmans, S. A. Y., & Payne, J. (2012). *The healthy mind platter*. NeuroLeadership Journal, 4, 1–23.
https://repository.uantwerpen.be/link/irua/169061

26   McKinsey Health Institute. (2025, January 16). *Thriving workplaces: How employers can improve productivity and change lives*. McKinsey & Company.
https://www.mckinsey.com/mhi/media-center/new-report-reinforces-the-social-and-economic-benefits-of-investing-in-employee-health

27   Grasso-Cladera, A., Arenas-Perez, M., Wegertseder-Martinez, P., Vilina, E., Mattoli-Sanchez, J., & Parada, F. J. (2025). *Neuroscientific insights into the built environment: A systematic review of indoor environmental quality and psychological wellbeing*. International Journal of Environmental Research and Public Health, 22(6), 824.
https://doi.org/10.3390/ijerph22060824

28   Guidi, J. et al. (2021). Allostatic load and its impact on health: A systematic review. *Psychotherapy and Psychosomatics, 90*(1), 11–27.
https://doi.org/10.1159/000510696

29   Dattani, S., Rodés-Guirao, L., Ritchie, H., & Roser, M. (2023). *Mental health.* **Our World in Data**.
https://ourworldindata.org/mental-health

30   World Health Organization. (2025). *Over a billion people living with mental health conditions – services require urgent scale-up*.
https://www.who.int/news/item/02-09-2025-over-a-billion-people-living-with-mental-health-conditions-services-require-urgent-scale-up

31   GBD 2019 Mental Disorders Collaborators. (2022). *Global, regional, and national burden of 12 mental disorders in 204 countries and territories, 1990–2019: A systematic analysis for the Global Burden of Disease Study 2019. The Lancet Psychiatry, 9*(2), 137–150.
https://doi.org/10.1016/S2215-0366(21)00395-3

32   Vigo, D., Thornicroft, G., & Atun, R. (2016). *Estimating the true global burden of mental illness. The Lancet Psychiatry, 3*(2), 171–178.
https://doi.org/10.1016/S2215-0366(15)00505-2

33   Lisa Worksheets. (n.d.). What is the window of tolerance and why is it so important?
https://lisaworksheets.com/p/what-is-the-window-of-tolerance-and-why-is-it-so-important.html

34   Siegel, D. J. (1999). *The developing mind: Toward a neurobiology of interpersonal experience*. Guilford Press.

35   Davis, E. (n.d.). *The intersection of masculinity and workplace culture: What are we missing?* Erin Davis Co.
https://www.erindavisco.ca/equity-diversity-and-inclusion-resources/the-intersection-of-masculinity-and-workplace-culture-what-are-we-missing

36   Litherland, S., Miller, P., & Hyder, S. (2025). What is masculinity in a contemporary Australian context? *Journal of Men's Health*, 21(2), 58–66.
https://doi.org/10.22514/jomh.2025.022

37   Joseph Levy Foundation. (2021, March 10). Voicebox drama workshops. https://www.jlf.org.uk/news/2021/voicebox-drama-workshops

38   Khanam, S., & Ishrat, A. (2024). A study of challenges faced by women in leadership role. *International Journal for Multidisciplinary Research, 6*(2), 1–10. https://doi.org/gtsnt7

39   Eareckson, H. B., & Heilman, M. E. (2024). Explaining penalties and rewards for gender norm violations: A unified theory. *Sex Roles.* https://doi.org/10.1007/s11199-024-01540-8

40   UN Women. (2022). *Intersectionality resource guide and toolkit: An intersectional approach to leave no one behind.* United Nations Entity for Gender Equality and the Empowerment of Women. https://unwomen.org.au/publications-and-resources/intersectionality-resource-guide-and-toolkit/

41   Torres, A. J. C., et al. (2024). The impact of motherhood on women's career progression: A scoping review of evidence-based interventions. *Behavioral Sciences, 14*(4), 275. https://giwl.anu.edu.au/our-research/impact-motherhood-womens-career-progression

42   UN Women. (2022). *Intersectionality resource guide and toolkit*

43   Sun, Y., & Billsberry, J. (2024). *What is this thing called misfit? A systematic review into how employee misfit has been defined and researched.* Management Review Quarterly, 75, 3263–3326. https://doi.org/10.1007/s11301-024-00461-w

44   Krekel, C., Ward, G., & De Neve, J.-E. (2020). *Employee wellbeing, productivity, and firm performance: Evidence and case studies.* Harvard Business School. https://papers.ssrn.com/sol3/papers.cfm?abstract_id=3356581

45   Qamar, F., Afshan, G., & Rana, S. A. (2023). Sustainable HRM and wellbeing: Systematic review and future research agenda. *Management Review Quarterly, 74,* 2289–2339. https://doi.org/10.1007/s11301-023-00360-6

46   Kumprang, K., & Suriyankietkaew, S. (2024). Mechanisms of organisational mindfulness on employee wellbeing and engagement: A multi-level analysis. *Administrative Sciences, 14*(6), 121. https://doi.org/10.3390/admsci14060121

47   Zhang, H., Sun, W., & Tang, G. (2024). Relational leadership and work–life balance: The moderated mediating role of relational energy. *Asia Pacific Journal of Management.* https://doi.org/10.1007/s10490-024-09995-9

48   Lawrence, J., Rasche, A., & Kenny, K. (2018). Sustainability as opportunity: Unilever's Sustainable Living Plan. In *Managing Sustainable Business* (435–455). Springer. https://doi.org/10.1007/978-94-024-1144-7_21

49   Arslan, A. M., Wang, H. W., & Rahman, A. U. (2025). Exploring the relationship between adaptive organisational behaviour, innovation, and employee mental health: A case study of Unilever's Sustainable Living Plan. *Journal of Human Resource and Sustainability Studies, 13*(1), 40–52.
https://doi.org/10.4236/jhrss.2025.131003

50   Tan, K. H. (2025). *Integrating sustainability into the corporate strategy: A critical analysis of Unilever's Sustainable Living Plan.* Graham International University.
https://doi.org/10.13140/RG.2.2.20946.47040

51   Aristotle. (1998). *Physics* (R. P. Hardie & R. K. Gaye, Trans.). Oxford University Press.
http://classics.mit.edu/Aristotle/physics.html
(Original work published ca. 350 BCE)

52   Keele, K. D., & Roberts, J. (1983). *Leonardo da Vinci: Anatomical drawings from the Royal Library, Windsor Castle.* The Metropolitan Museum of Art.
https://www.metmuseum.org/met-publications/leonardo-da-vinci-anatomi-cal-drawings-from-the-royal-library-windsor-castle

53   Descartes, R. (1948). *The passions of the soul.* In W. Dennis (Ed.), *Readings in the history of psychology* (pp. 25–31). Appleton-Century-Crofts.
https://psycnet.apa.org/record/2006-10213-004 (Original work published 1650)

54   Carmichael, L. (1926). Sir Charles Bell: A contribution to the history of physio-logical psychology. *Psychological Review, 33*(3), 188–217.
https://doi.org/10.1037/h0072659

55   Bongaardt, R., & Meijer, O. G. (2000). Bernstein's theory of movement behav-ior: Historical development and contemporary relevance. *Journal of Motor Behavior, 32*(1), 57–71.
https://doi.org/10.1080/00222890009601360

56   Zou, L., et al. (2018). Effects of mind–body exercises (tai chi/yoga) on heart rate variability parameters and perceived stress: A systematic review with meta-analysis. *Journal of Clinical Medicine, 7*(11), 404.
https://www.mdpi.com/2077-0383/7/11/404

57   Gruman, J. A., & Choi, E. (2021). *Wellbeing at work: A balanced approach to positive organisational studies.* In S. Dhiman (Ed.), *The Palgrave handbook of workplace wellbeing* (pp. 169–207). Palgrave Macmillan.
https://link.springer.com/rwe/10.1007/978-3-030-02470-3_84-1

58   Umoh, R. (2018, August 23). *The meeting hack loved by CEOs at Google, Facebook and LinkedIn.* CNBC.
https://www.cnbc.com/2018/08/23/why-ceos-at-google-facebook-and-linke-din-love-walking-meetings.html

59   Salesforce wellbeing program context ("B-Well Together" wellbeing sessions): Salesforce. (n.d.). *Employee health and wellbeing.*
https://www.salesforce.com/resources/future-of-work/employ-ee-health-and-wellbeing/

60   Microsoft. (n.d.). *Ergonomics* (Microsoft Benefits).
https://usbenefits.microsoft.com/us/en/ergonomics.html

[61] Wang, C., Dai, Y., Yang, Y., Yuan, X., Zhang, M., Zeng, J., Zhong, X., Meng, J., & Jiang, C. (2023). *Effects of Tai Chi on working memory in older adults: Evidence from combined fNIRS and ERP*. Frontiers in Aging Neuroscience, 15, 1206891. https://doi.org/10.3389/fnagi.2023.1206891

[62] Calderone, A., Latella, D., Impellizzeri, F., de Pasquale, P., Famà, F., Quartarone, A., & Calabrò, R. S. (2024). Neurobiological changes induced by mindfulness and meditation: A systematic review. *Biomedicines, 12*(11), 2613. https://doi.org/10.3390/biomedicines12112613

[63] Hartkamp, M., & Thornton, I. M. (2017). Meditation, cognitive flexibility and wellbeing. *Journal of Cognitive Enhancement, 1,* 182–196. https://doi.org/10.1007/s41465-017-0026-3 [link.springer.com]

[64] Wixted, J., & Cai, D. J. (2013). Memory consolidation. In *The Oxford Handbook of Cognitive Neuroscience, Volume 1: Core Topics* (436–455). Oxford University Press. https://doi.org/10.1093/oxfordhb/9780199988693.013.0021

[65] Ratey, J. J., & Hagerman, E. (2008). *Spark: The revolutionary new science of exercise and the brain*. Little, Brown and Co.

[66] Kabat-Zinn, J. (1994). *Wherever you go, there you are: Mindfulness meditation in everyday life*. Hyperion.

[67] Lutz, A., Slagter, H. A., Dunne, J. D., & Davidson, R. J. (2008). Attention regulation and monitoring in meditation. *Trends in Cognitive Sciences, 12*(4), 163–169. https://doi.org/10.1016/j.tics.2008.01.005

[68] Tang, Y.-Y., Hölzel, B. K., & Posner, M. I. (2015). The neuroscience of mindfulness meditation. *Nature Reviews Neuroscience, 16*(4), 213–225 https://doi.org/10.1038/nrn3916

[69] Guidi, J., Lucente, M., Sonino, N., & Fava, G. A. (2021). Allostatic load and its impact on health: A systematic review. *Psychotherapy and Psychosomatics, 90*(1), 11–27. https://doi.org/10.1159/000510696

[70] McCrory, C., et al. (2023). Towards a consensus definition of allostatic load: A multi-cohort, multi-system, multi-biomarker individual participant data (IPD) meta-analysis. *Psychoneuroendocrinology, 153*, 106117. https://doi.org/10.1016/j.psyneuen.2023.106117

[71] Rosemberg, M. A. S., Granner, J., Li, Y., & Seng, J. S. (2020). A scoping review of interventions targeting allostatic load. *Stress, 23*(5), 519–528. https://doi.org/10.1080/10253890.2020.1784136

[72] Pfaltz, M. C., & Schnyder, U. (2023). Allostatic load and allostatic overload: Preventive and clinical implications. *Psychotherapy and Psychosomatics, 92*(5), 279–282. https://doi.org/10.1159/000534340

[73] Xie, Y., Liu, S., Chen, X., Yu, H., Yang, Y., & Wang, W. (2021). *Effects of exercise on sleep quality and insomnia in adults: A systematic review and meta-analysis of randomized controlled trials*. Frontiers in Psychiatry, 12, Article 664499. https://doi.org/10.3389/fpsyt.2021.664499

[74] D'Alessio, L., et al. (2020). Reducing allostatic load in depression and anxiety disorders: Physical activity and yoga practice as add-on therapies. *Frontiers in Psychiatry, 11*, Article 501. https://doi.org/10.3389/fpsyt.2020.00501

[75] Csikszentmihalyi, M. (1990). Flow: *The psychology of optimal experience.* Harper & Row.

[76] Dietrich, A. (2004). Neurocognitive mechanisms underlying the experience of flow. *Consciousness and Cognition, 13*(4), 746–761. https://doi.org/10.1016/j.concog.2004.07.002

[77] Kurhaluk, N., Kołodziejska, R., Kamiński, P., & Tkaczenko, H. (2025). Integrative neuroimmune role of the parasympathetic nervous system, vagus nerve and gut microbiota in stress modulation: A narrative review. *International Journal of Molecular Sciences, 26*(23), 11706. https://www.mdpi.com/1422-0067/26/23/11706

[78] Ackland, G. L., Patel, A. B. U., Miller, S., et al. (2025). Non-invasive vagus nerve stimulation and exercise capacity in healthy volunteers: A randomized trial. *European Heart Journal, 46*(17), 1634–1644. https://doi.org/10.1093/eurheartj/ehaf037

[79] Guy-Evans, O., & McLeod, S. (2025). Hypothalamic–Pituitary–Adrenal (HPA) Axis. *Simply Psychology.* https://www.simplypsychology.org/hypothalamic-pituitary-adrenal-axis.html

[80] Sterling, C. (2024). *Why neuroscience is key to workplace wellbeing.* Wellbeing Think Tank. https://www.wellbeingthinktank.org/blog/why-neuroscience-matters-for-workplace-wellbeing

[81] Headrick, L., Newman, D. A., Park, Y. A., & Liang, Y. (2023). Recovery experiences for work and health outcomes: A meta-analysis and recovery-engagement-exhaustion model. **Journal of Business and** Psychology, 38, 821–864 https://doi.org/10.1007/s10869-022-09821-3

[82] Rogers, A., Brady, P., & Roberts, D. (2025). *Building a neuro-inclusive workplace.* The Scholarly Kitchen. https://scholarlykitchen.sspnet.org/2025/03/17/building-a-neuro-inclusive-workplace/

[83] Ataya, A. (2024). Sensory ergonomics: Designing inclusive workspaces for neurodiversity. *Journal of Ergonomics, 14*(6). https://www.longdom.org/open-access/sensory-ergonomics-designing-inclusive-workspaces-for-neurodiversity-1100929.html

[84] Trenz, N., & Keith, N. (2024). Promoting new habits at work through implementation intentions. Journal of Occupational and Organizational Psychology, 97(4), 1813–1834 https://doi.org/10.1111/joop.12540

[85] Rudy, B. C. (2022, July 11). *Build learning into your employees' workflow.* Harvard Business Review. https://hbr.org/2022/07/build-learning-into-your-employees-workflow

86 World Health Organization. (2021). *Comprehensive mental health action plan 2013–2030*. World Health Organization. https://www.who.int/publications/i/item/9789240031029

87 Atlassian. (2024, February 18). *Psychological safety at work: What it is, why it matters, and how to build it.* Work Life by Atlassian. https://www.atlassian.com/blog/teamwork/what-does-psychological-safe-ty-mean-anyway

88 Edmondson, A. C. (2019). *The fearless organization: Creating psychological safety in the workplace for learning, innovation, and growth.* Wiley.

89 Society for Human Resource Management. (2025, October 20). *Stack ranking: The hidden cost of the easy way out.* https://www.shrm.org/enterprise-solutions/insights/stack-ranking-hidden-cost-of-easy-way-out

90 Nkone, B., Matoka, C., & Ngirwa, C. (2025). *Effect of employee morale on successful implementation of strategic plans in the public sector.* International Research Journal of Economics and Management Studies, 4(1), 58–67. https://irjems.org/Volume-4-Issue-1/IRJEMS-V4I1P107.pdf

91 Krekel, C., Ward, G., & De Neve, J.-E. (2019). *Employee wellbeing, productivity, and firm performance.* In Global happiness and wellbeing policy report (pp. 72–94). Sustainable Development Solutions Network. https://www.hbs.edu/ris/Publication%20Files/gh19_ch5_9e171d71-db54-4e08-a2eb-3cf1587daf4a.pdf

92 Likierman, A. (2025, November 29). *Why human judgement is essential in the age of AI.* London Business School. https://www.london.edu/think/human-judgement-essential-in-ai

93 Rath, T., & Harter, J. (2010). *Wellbeing: The five essential elements.* Gallup Press

94 Jarden, R. J., Siegert, R. J., Koziol-McLain, J., Bujalka, H., & Sandham, M. H. (2023). Wellbeing measures for workers: A systematic review and methodological quality appraisal. *Frontiers in Public Health, 11*, 1053179. https://doi.org/10.3389/fpubh.2023.1053179

95 Purcell, J. (2024). *Case study: SAP shows how employee wellbeing boosts the bottom line.* SIYLI. https://siyli.org/resources/case-studies/case-study-sap-shows-how-employ-ee-wellbeing-boosts-the-bottom-line

96 Chylinski, M. (2024). *The Salesforce Approach to Mental Wellness: A Blue-print for Success and Growth.* LinkedIn. https://www.linkedin.com/pulse/salesforce-approach-mental-wellness-blue-print-success-manya-chylinski-txrqf

97 De Neve, J.-E., Kaats, M., & Ward, G. (2024). *Workplace wellbeing and firm performance.* University of Oxford Wellbeing Research Centre Working Paper Series. https://doi.org/10.5287/ora-bpkbjayvk

98   Edmondson, A. C., & Bransby, D. P. (2023). *Psychological safety comes of age: Observed themes in an established literature.* Annual Review of Organizational Psychology and Organizational Behavior, 10, 55–78.
https://doi.org/10.1146/annurev-orgpsych-120920-055217

99   World Health Organization. (2024). *Mental health and psychosocial support in workplace settings: Guidance for organisations.*
https://www.who.int/publications/i/item/9789240057944

100   Purcell, J. (2024). *Case study: SAP*

101   Chylinski, M. (2024). *The Salesforce Approach to Mental Wellness*

102   De Neve, J.-E., Kaats, M., & Ward, G. (2024). *Workplace wellbeing and firm performance.*